DAILIES
&
RUSHES

DAILIES & RUSHES

BY SUSAN KINSOLVING

GROVE PRESS
NEW YORK

Published simultaneously in Canada
Printed in the United States of America

FIRST EDITION

Library of Congress Cataloging-in-Publication Data

Kinsolving, Susan.
    Dailies & rushes / Susan Kinsolving.
        p.   cm.
    ISBN 0-8021-3605-2
    I. Title.   II. Title: Dailies and rushes.
PS3561.I578D35   1999
811'.54—dc21   98-43409

Design by Julie Duquet

Grove Press
841 Broadway
New York, NY 10003

00 01 02   10 9 8 7 6 5 4 3

Acknowledgments

My thanks to the editors of the following magazines and anthologies in which some of these poems previously appeared:

Antioch Review, The Beloit Poetry Journal, Boogie Woogie Review, Connecticut Quarterly, Connecticut River Review, Dideann, Ellipsis, G. W. Review, Grand Street, Harvard Magazine, High Plains Review, The Nation, The New Republic, The Paris Review, Press, The Register Citizen, Shenandoah, Slant, The Texas Review, Washout Review, West Branch, Western Humanities Review.

All Nations Poetry Anthology (Triton College Press), *Articulations: Poetry About Illness and the Body* (University of Iowa Press); *Contemporary New England Poetry: A Sampler* (Texas Review Press); *From the Hudson to the World; Voices of the River* (Hudson River Sloop Clearwater, Inc.); *To Woo & to Wed* (Poseidon Press, Simon & Schuster). Some early poems were published under the name Susan Baumann.

To Richard Howard, man of letters, mentor, and marvel, my greatest gratitude.

I appreciate the encouragement and support offered to me by The Connecticut Commission on the Arts, The Ragdale Foundation, and The Corporation of Yaddo.

Joan Bingham, Carol Franc Buck, David Carlson, Arthur Kovacs, Dale Loy, Elizabeth MacDonald, Nion McEvoy, Cathy Mellett, Cynthia Sears, Geraldine Stutz, William O. Walker, Susan York, and Ann Zeff are among the friends who believe in the muse and me. I thank them all.

When I was a child, my mother, Catharine Dewey Baumann, read many poems to me and took me to meet Carl Sandburg and Kenneth Rexroth.

For Tuie & William
at different times, in different places

Contents

On the Poems of Susan Kinsolving

It is enjoyable, it is edifying too, observing this new poet articulate, in the sequence of poems she so tellingly entitles according to quotidian processes and contact highs that have their cinematic *passage* in the two nouns, Dailies and Rushes; it is above all comforting (to our craving for the coherences of art) to trace with her, in poem after poem, the curve upward out of mere and sheer wit, making the rising discovery that words together can rouse and, so to speak, raid their message even as they report it *on the line:*

> . . . borders gone wild
> with weeds, stark staring asters, blackest black-eyed Susans,
> aluminum cans, butts, and bottles.

Asters, cans, butts—this Susan carries her puns lightly enough to parry her contemporary uneasiness about rhyme, which will usually avoid being terminal, just as her gift for enjambment will encourage her to avoid the line of self-help:

> My newest experience is my oldest
> fear. Everything here is at the
> edge.

Reading such lines aloud without seeing what she has done by folding them over the margin is some indication of the fine ear and the finer wit, which operates against the expectations of decorum by *another* decorum, the obligations of irony.

And then the curve of the new poet's accomplishment moves beyond wit to observation, the second discovery that words are not only at work among themselves but that they afford information (frequently the most reliable we have, for the eye wearies and the ear weakens, and the nose was never wide awake) about the world out there. As an earnest of that world, often enough, Susan Kinsolving is in a field, surrounded by mysteries that her words must—or may—solve. She is very good at coaxing the presences to manifest themselves—quite different from the absent poetics of our missing master Mark Strand, who so famously reported that in a field—remember?— he is the absence of field. Susan Kinsolving lets the presences of what is going on in the field replace her, stand in for her own being-there, and so her new poems tell us quite a lot about the world of fields, before they tell us about her:

> . . . Wandering through
> our fields, we found the bones
> of a deer, the skin of a snake,
> old apples, brittle thistles.
> Torn with the last red berry,
> my hand bled into your mouth.

But they do, of course—all these poems of critical pastoral, of cross-grained profusion—tell us eventually about the poet; indeed, she rises out of wit and observation into her passionately earned identity, the consequence of much hard looking—inward. When I speak, as I am eager to do, of the "new" poet among us, I mean of course that she is new *to us,* for as Emerson remarked in another context altogether, there must have been a long foreground to a poetry that is as skillful as all this, one of the marks of such skill being her willingness to leave out the signs of effort, the stigmata of endeavor. Nothing can be easy that parades such ease as this:

> As a stunted woman (you might say
> stunt) my body is everyday
> ready to explode in some crazy way.
> My breasts feel wired, patched with squibs.
> I'll take bruises, cuts, a few cracked ribs.

Remarkable how Susan Kinsolving can make a song out of almost anything. It must have something to do with those preparations, those secret doings (and undoings) around the pot, over the fire: we are being told here what can be made up, made out, made over. She is, as a poet must be, a true maker. Just listen, just look!

RICHARD HOWARD

WINTER WATCH

THE GIFT

In red foil paper was my present, just
as I had asked: a magnifying glass. I
was five, but my dismay was huge
intensified by feigned gratitude. What
to say? Where was the word of my mis-
take? In silence, I enlarged snow-
flakes, pine needles, carpet threads, six
crumbs of cake, and the dark pupils
of my dog's eyes. But the word hid
elsewhere, almost disguised, as glass
might be the illusion of clarity. And so
it's been in all my words and hopes:
poems, the elusive gift, the microscope.

WITHOUT

I saw a stick
wandering over snowdrifts
cheerful and unassuming
twirling and unarmed.

A Chaplin cane without Charlie
wobbled and poked
making its way
taking its walk alone
a crutch without connection.

It plodded deep
half disappearing in white
while creating and leaving
the shape of its emptiness.

I followed it far
an odd extension I could not grasp
and it went away,

an immaculate line of idea
on which only cold air
was allowed to lean.

SNOW SLEEP

As icicles fell between
the edge of the eave and the night,
my grandmother fell
into what she said was "snow
sleep." The clear points of her

consciousness broke down
into drifts and entered shapes
unseen. The blue flakes
of her old eyes opened
into an absolute. Whiteness

covered over my grandmother
and under the sheets
of those December weeks,
she was deeper than seasons,
she was calmer than cold.

CUBES ON A CURVE

White cubes on a white curve are snow-covered
hives on a snow-covered hill. Walking past
this icy pasture, I hear a hum, a low minor

one, thin as the crystalline lace in the ditch,
distant as the reasons shaping the drift. Who
can come to grips with insects or ice, other

worlds in this? In the inner ear is what
buzzes here. And beyond. I cannot see, but
in the white box is a frozen bee. Clover

catches its breath and sap stops in the trees. Hands
warm as they numb. Gradually, quietly,
momentous forces reduce to minute

degrees. Hope is as elementary as
ancient mercury. Finally, each hum
is nothing but a prayer for one, this one.

FROM DECEMBER TO FEBRUARY

The depth of cold, that bone and tooth of winter, stuns us
as the immensity of ice snaps and settles over the jagged
river, its current turned into a disorder of edges. Only
our senses converge as we stare in silence unable to ask

what holds us here with the wind biting our lips, our gloved
fingertips, numbing us with something sub-zero, a negative
count toward infinity. Last night, the knife points of stars
stopped us from walking into the warmth of a room. Instead,

we stood shivering as if waiting for the black water-taffeta
sky to be slit open, for the silver light to pour out, kindle
its color, and release us from so much space, from the vast
chill of separation, the force of isolation. Even the moon

denied its radiant cradle and suspended a steely scythe.
But we who were born in this season have learned the myths
of its severity, its impervious heart. We will walk
by the river and into the night together. After all, we were

once the infants suited for this frosted earth and frozen air.
We became the children who accepted the chilblains of their own
creations, their small arms feathered with soft flakes, their bodies
lying in an imitation of angels, as ours lie in another shape.

PEELINGS

What is the matter here, but a hearty way
to stew and get through another winter?
The porcelain basin is layered, a cross-
hatching of tattered wet ribbons, earth
orange, dirt brown, root white, the thin
skins that separate space from the heart
of the matter. With the sinews of carrot,
the fortitude of potato, the perseverance
of parsnip, a person can pare down an enigma.
What is unresolved can dissolve, lost
in the broth of seasons. With so many
mouths to feed, so much pith and peeling,
what is the recipe for comfort in our vast
cold? What changes this chill to a fast boil?

BREAKAGE

OUR FIELDS

With the dog panting beside
us, still we could not equate
earth or even approximate
an animal. Wandering through
our fields, we found the bones
of a deer, the skin of a snake,
old apples, brittle thistles.
Torn with the last red berry,
my hand bled into your mouth.

A cloud covered where we stood
and you left for a long walk
in the woods. I slept, legs
apart, in autumn's warmest bed
until you returned and said,
"The trees need to be cleared;
they must not grow any thicker"
(or we shall never get through
them together). A hawk made rings

above. . . . I thought of excesses
of love and how they too require
thinning, trimming. But that was
in September's fire; by November,
we began to tire. Death was near
to us that season; we learned to
see its beauty and its reason. We
let each other grow as self, then
each of us changed into someone else.

WALKING AFTER WINTER

Following bright bloodroot
over our thawing land,
we survey old fence posts
and how they finally stand.

One turns in the stream bed
pulling from spring's wake;
another leans into barbed wire
denying a splitting break.

Beside our tortured apple tree
broken from its full yield
more fencing has collapsed
opening forest to field.

Although our long barbed edge
will never be repaired,
we walk calmly over each
raw acre we have shared.

The broken stakes and torn
tree fuse into a sign
as we continue up our hill,
refusing to resign

until we overlook the valley
and the borders of our farm;
then we face each other
and know the winter's harm.

LEAVING

Your strategy is persistence, proceeding
like the first edge
of moon, late in the day. The evidence
continues almost
imperceptibly, thin as porcelain, clear
as spider strands,
until we are in the same room, the same
bed, with arms
binding our bodies, your tongue in my
mouth begins to say
separate words. I know you are moving
delicately, distantly,
away. Soon you become as elusive as dust
in air, circular as
the hem of my silken sleeve, and secret
as old poisonous
recipes. Slowly, I start to see that you
are isinglass over
an incinerator. Betrayal cracks the back
of a sacred book.
Pain is sharp; white cells are attacking
my heart as you
open the door glancing a look in the hall
mirror, at a mask
of deceit, a conspirator holding a prepacked
suitcase, anxious
not to be late for someone you have to meet.

WALKING BACK

What could be truer than this summation
of summer: an edge of the interstate in August?
You've driven away over the asphalt
leaving me to find a way back across a surface

shimmering with heat, its borders gone wild
with weeds, stark staring asters, blackest black-eyed Susans,
aluminum cans, butts, and bottles. Here
I move among the discards where smoke and liquid leave

their shards, where blue chicory and Dixie
cups dry in erosion's sand, where disregard is strewn
with speed by hand, where neglect frees the land.
What could be truer than this summation of summer?

SNARLS

From the fields, he braids his way into my nap
with a careful count of our hay. Mindful, I
stand behind his chair and remove bits of straw

from his tangled blond hair. He tells me each
bale must pay the property taxes, but he weights
the thinnest straw to burden me until we split

hairs for property. I stare at his crooked part.
I comb through the broken bits until, distressed,
I stand apart. I warn him of the darkness

of my locks. He leans toward the table and laughs
at a knife crossing the circle of a plate. Then,
he shakes his head, laughs again, and I wake.

IN PREPARATION

The mind leaves
before the suitcase is fully packed.
All day I take the last
turn off our road. In the rearview
mirror, I see the trees
descend, the house diminish, the roof
disappear. I leave our keys
first on the table, then in a drawer,
later in a dish by the door.
I watch the water run from our faucet
and the panes of light shift
across our floor. When I was a child,
moving scared me; every time
I located my life, it wandered away once
more. I dreamed of fortune-
tellers, wide-eyed, who covered my ears
with their hands and whispered
unspeakable words. In the silence of this
room, repeatedly, I hear
the closing door, as it has never closed before.

WRITING YOU OF WESSEX

Remember the time I told you how the true heart
of Thomas Hardy
was buried in the Dorset countryside while
his ashes were kept

at Westminster? Remember how matter-of-fact
you answered that
the heart's extraction once had been common practice?
It was in that split

second, I wanted to tell you how my heart is
cut out and buried
in your heart, which I love; except for the fact, I
am buried alive

in this throbbing entombment. And I am frantic
for nothing escapes
this encasement, nothing divides this too deep two-
beat rhythm, deadly

in its music, artful in its making of ash
and intimacy.
Hardy knew the binding of love's horrible blade.
Deep in his divided

heart, he severed hope from healing, predicting
how I come apart
with you and still remain, wanting and writing once
again, foolhardy.

SEQUINS

What I wear, wears on you so darkly.

> In spangled light,
> I am recondite.

Bright discs of color satisfy my skin,
ornament this surface of self, and flash a million meteors
across your dusty mirror. These are my mermaid's scales
for which I weighed the worth of my worn dress. Yes,
these tiny gaudy gleams are why I shed my sensible
shoes and pointed my toes to fit the dazzling idea
of this tale. Shimmering in this rare reflective glare,
I hear the siren who has come to alarm and enlighten you.
Call this cheap costuming or an epidermal illusion
full of foolishness, but know that something in this sheen
is suiting me. Cell by cell, this change wears well. Sequin
by sequin, beware of how I glisten

> and what I wear.
> Beware. . . .

PARTING GIFT

Here. Take these. My red beads. Call them the bright berries
I cannot crush in your mouth. Or the embers left
unsorted from the axis of our ash, small spheres
of desire that hung hope, an amulet and rope,
from my neck. Yes, you must have all these . . . red beads.

My rosary of regard, my scarlet penance
for your crimson charm, these blood beads rushed artery
into brain and back again pounding my chambered
heart without reprieve until I wore it on my sleeve.
Take these from me. Touch each one carefully. Plastic

cheap and ruby rich, these hard revolutions turn
the small rondure in which I burn. In your pocket,
keep this strand. Press each match head of redness into
your hand. Then snap the string in two, scattering red
beads, releasing me from the circumference of you.

BASEMENT

My newest experience is my oldest
fear. Everything here is at the
edge. This room is at the edge
of the sea; it is an edge for me.

What hurt me once still hurts me
now. My losses: I lost rural acres,
a house, a life. I left a husband;
I lost my past as he lost his wife.

Now I go from waves to undertow
here at the ocean's cliffs. How
does a distant farmhouse find
me? How is it that I drift away

from windows framing the sea
until I'm there, sitting on a stair
where all is underground? The ocean
makes no sound in a cellar of stone.

In that cool cavity of memory, I see
how achingly we made our concrete
mix, in which we set a furnace
and wrote our names with sticks.

Unearthed scenes fill my skull, as
gray cement covers a white seagull.
In old sacks, onions sleep. Artesian
water drips in silty leaks; a shelf

creaks with harvests in Mason jars.
In the presence of pale pears and
the deadened red of rhubarb, I hover
on those stairs. Far from the warmth

of sun on sand, I reach for a banister,
some way to grip and understand this
unfathomable edge: this pain even waves
can't dredge, the unspoken. Husband,

hear me haunting those dusty steps?
Remember, I swept the floors above
in this house restored and destroyed
by love? With dark cries, I wept at how

we undermined more than this basement
could confine. As living rooms and bed-
rooms split apart, we tore off all
the flesh of home and gnawed each

other down to bone. I took heart
in cellar stones and let earth restrain
the cracks of our base incisions. Dirt
was my deep philosopher, rooted in

divisions. Tender with moss, indurate
with stone, earth insists on entering
the human abyss. Waiting by each wall
were humus, gravel, and loam, ready

for the grave underneath our home.
On this tidal ledge, waves of confusion
roar; the past returns again crashing
as before. From beach to basement,

I vacillate, unable to locate the rough-
hewn cellar door. Its light-fringed
edge led up to the lawn, but even more
it admitted the departure, I endure.

LOCK AND KEY

The room is empty. I know and don't care;
away from the window, I've turned my chair.

The door is closed. No light can come in.
On the table is an apple, half eaten.

On the desk, your note says "I have one doubt
and . . ." Other words have been rubbed out.

Tomorrow the lily will begin to bloom,
a white extravagance in a darkened room.

The clock is still ticking, but slowing with time;
today it began showing an eight for a nine.

A glass full of water was left by the bed.
The air will drink it with the thirst of the dead.

The lily will wilt and the apple will rot.
Worms may evolve. Probably not.

You are not missed in that sealed room.
A monument to absence, it is our tomb.

SHADES OF GREEN

Three thousand miles from
here, I stood at dawn
on the edge between an uncut
field and a mowed lawn.

That half acre aligned
its blades of division;
tangled to the roots, I
entwined miles of decision.

Shaken by winds, bitter
seed crowns fell;
suspicion covered the field
and tillage grew to tell.

Sorrow foraged the lawn
stripping the sweet beds bare.
Nightshade entangled clover
as I stalked past despair.

The yard lay green and ruled,
a half-truth of order
against the unruly weeds;
my anger cut its border.

At noon, I departed
with the line I'd drawn.
The pasture is still present,
but now the edge is gone.

ADMISSION OF TWO

Old enough
to be brief and grant permission

they began
with each other again.

He admitted that for him

it was a yellow brick house
torn and crumbling
by the Indiana Turnpike.

She said that for her

it was the swarming and swooping
of pigeon flocks
on Houston Street.

Then he said that all along he had thought

it was the morning for her
in the Southwest
when the car would not start.

No she sighed
it was the swooping of those birds
between the buildings
on Houston Street.

A BRIDE AGAIN

When I am a bride again
I will carry water
lilies and at the altar
there will be three urns,
one of ash
another of air
and the third will be of earth.

There will be no water
for the lilies or for me.
We will move in an arid dream
of white dust and lace, a ritual
nightmare in which all
the solitude and sway of our long
stems will be broken
again.

I will lift my veil
and the lilies will close,
for there is no water
in marriage, only blood.

SOTTO VOCE

No one has touched me for months, maybe now it is
years. When a mere cashier touches my hand, placing change
in my palm, my heart leaps, a small sissonne of spirit.
I show a doctor where I ache and follow his eyes
until they turn into cool instruments. No one else
enjoys waiting in line, the breath of strangers nearing
the neck. But I stand waiting. I stare. And I admit
to such depravation. A plum has made me shudder
with gratitude, its soft flesh so giving, its juices
running without regard. I could not help myself. No.
I ate plums until I was sick, reaching for more. More.

OTHER WORLDS

THE NIGHT NURSE

Disguised as the night nurse, the censor is
administering my medicine and assuring me
that my sleep will not be of my own making.
My demons, she says, are a disease that may
be prevented, though never cured. She begins

to remove the books from my bedstand. She
rewrites my prescriptions, tears my letters,
and pinches off the rose that leans out
of my water glass. Then she flushes the ink
from my pen. She straightens the sheet

so that it falls over my mouth and nose. As
she pulls one corner taut, she cajoles, "You'll
feel better if you lie still. Your thoughts
need rest; doctor knows best." She counts from
one to ten, one to ten again, and injects.

"These are your numbers," she soothes. "You must
not refuse. The hospital provides them free
of charge and we can insert them without leaving
scars. Accept them as a gift, unless you prefer
to be intravenously fed, but enough said." She

coaxes one to ten, one to ten again. I try to
hear the sounds. I search for my sustenance
of consonants and vowels. A black line moves
through me, numbing my tongue. As the syllables
of my dreams are blotted out, the nurse begins to shout.

WAITING THEM OUT

Placid and in a bathrobe, she is
sitting by the swimming pool and
watching the wind spread the water.

Restitution has riddled her to this,
last resort, the solace and comfort
of slight incongruities: cold air

on a sundeck, potted palms made
of plastic, sitting alone among chairs,
a diving board without a diver, dying

bored without a death. Imagine
the indulgence, all the riches reduced
to an extravagant ennui. "Not a cigarette

or a murdered infant could get a rise
out of that one," said the orderly, so
complacent with chaos and crafts.

There is a calm that shares its secret
with a shriek, a rat twitching through
its poisoned feast. Her mouse heart sobs.
Everything human has had its chance.

MASSES OF MARSH MARIGOLDS

Those were the words I brought
to bloom in my white confine,
a cell quaintly called "room."

Alliterative, mantra, cantata,
they meant to sparkle petals
over a stony stream, to move

consciousness back to babble
from scream. But the bruises
grew blue into black. The mind

a raw ransack, shattered bric-
a-brac, hospital two lips, no
sylvan or Plath. Well, nothing

stops it, each pretty outpouring
of blood, vomit, and shit. Woe,
I cried for my masses of marsh

marigolds to light like bright
finches in the broken branches
of my brain. Sob, beg. None came.

SAVING BINGE

I am on one again
wandering the raw pastures of Upstate
in want of redness,

gathering the last apples
the flaming rose hips
that hang from poor tatters of tree and bush.

What am I doing
but practicing my lover's advice?

He said
I would enjoy India
if my travels were somehow directed,

if for instance I searched
all over that curious continent
for blue buttons and cold spice.

PART ITALIAN

Like our summer landlady taking her inventory,
recording her saucers and scatti in that farmhouse
("modernized fifteenth century"), I kept accounts:
kilometers to Gubbio, notes on Signorelli, and

how many days the girasoli turned their heads
until light circled into memory. In that lively
language with so many pasts, time tensed by degrees.
My tutor said, "Verbs can be hypotheses." Thus,

one syllable of change might turn ancient lava
flows into souvenir bits of tufo. Another might replant
July's wheat field with August tobacco. The present
is conditional near a remote and perfect past. So how

does the foreigner depict the inarticulate? Small talk
turns to viper kits, extra virgin olive oil, Umbria's
dry soil, and the way Communists and Christians remain
so loyal. With bread ovens, fireflies, and afternoons

of doubt, the summer burned and flickered out. Warm
sleeves waved limply from the laundry line and the last
blossoms left the trumpet vine. At a stone sill with half
a glass of Classico, I tasted half-truths, all I could know.

IN VENICE READING ABOUT CAMBODIA
1979

Beside us, the black hulls glide,
close as caskets, an arm's length
away. Fingerlings spread through
dark reflections. All day, morning
news and sights confuse. Raw rice,
atrocious edicts, executions, and
The Eyeglasses Confiscation mix
with this Turner mist. Here, descent
is imperceptible, but cumulatively
clear. Beauty becomes bereavement,
sighing becomes a bridge. Saint Jerome
slays a dragon in dim paint-preserving
light; Harry's Bar serves eye-openers
for hangovers. Here, germ warfare,
ghettos, and mirrors were conceived.
All civilization shimmers with this air,
fetid as death camps, sweet as holidays.

HARARI TOWNSHIP DEPOT

One hawker has salve for night bugs.
Another has chicken baskets, but not a chicken.
Between slogans, a loudspeaker blares steel
drum music with static. Shrill sounds, raw sores,
filthy blankets make her at home in mango crates.
Cooking the gnarled yam over a little fire,
the old woman laughs. "The war don't never stop.
Who say we is safe, well, he a liar."

CONTAGIOUS MAGIC

The ones most in need of a revolution
are best at hiding
a broken shoelace, a kerchief, a lock
of hair, or if they are

very lucky, a tooth. Then they turn
the token into an agent
of revenge. Few are left with spirit
lively enough for practicing

this craft; most take up machines and
manifestos. But I knew one
woman so angry at evil that for fifteen
years she cursed the cuttings

from a dictator's fingernails. When
at last, his hands were
painfully paralyzed, she schemed to get
a scrap from his night-

shirt. She paid four silver coins to
a trembling laundry maid
for scorching off the piece that lay
closest to his heart.

For the next seven years, the old woman
concentrated on the cloth.
When an assassin shot through the dictator's
chest, so that his blood

blossomed on the palace walls like
crimson flowers, the woman
knew her work was done. She threw
the cloth into the fire and

prepared for the news to reach her
village. As the people,
laughing and weeping with joy, filled
the streets, she walked

among them with a large basket
filled with dried seeds,
bits of bone, small shells, smooth ·
stones, and curls of lambs'

wool. Pressing them into her
neighbors' hands, she said,
"Bear your spirits upon these.
Spirits will come to matter."

DANCE STEPS

When the world grew desperate enough, eccentric
solutions were attempted. The President started
xylophone lessons. Daily readings from Pushkin
and the I Ching opened Parliament. Every military
installation in Africa was required to maintain

a large aquarium. On alternate days, the Kremlin
became an infant day-care facility. Every Japanese
citizen wrote weekly to a Central American pen pal.
The Pope toured China and Australia to present Charlie
Chaplin film clips and vegetable gardening tips.

Of course, there was protest and cynicism, yet
undeniably things had changed. Newspapers reported
the details of foreign dreams. Summit meetings began
by swimming laps. Ancient Greek became the official
language of Mexico and Argentina. In Bombay, a luau

was given honoring Eskimos and televised by satellite
to Saudi Arabia. Exactly what resulted from all
these efforts was indeterminate; however, international
opinion favored further whims. Trees took on new stature.
Animals were consulted. Children held office. Romantic

love gained new respect. The gold standard broadened
to include well water, new jokes, and flower arranging.
Subsequently, values changed. Authority and innocence
merged. And it went on this way for a long time because
everyone wanted a better story with a happier ending.

THE REST

As murderers sleep
through the night with their hands
limp and open, the empress
snores with the soft wind coming
in the palace windows.

As soldiers and schoolgirls sleep
deeper than the dark
weary animals who curl into the dead
trees, the sick float past
their bloodstreams into an evening
of smooth lakes. As doors

do not creak and insects keep silent,
the watchdog is deaf to all
but his dreams. As infants forget that
they have left the womb,

the old forget that they are still
alive. As the longest night
endures, history closes its eyes
for the rest of the world.

PROTOCOL

Here is my arrangement
for the chairs.

I would like the chairs
scattered on the lawn
so that mountains may be seen
through their backs.

Mountains from miles away
will support spines
they cannot touch.

Then I shall drink
an octave out
of all my musical glasses.

I shall drink to the dorsal,
lumbar, sacral, caudal
Catskills, Adirondacks, and
to the High Sierras.

Cheers to the Rockies.
Here's to the Appalachians
and a toast to the Grand Tetons!

I shall stand and salute
the upright.

The glorious elevation
of mountains and vertebrae
is essentially

a seating arrangement.

PARTIAL PRAISE

A little mouthful of death is on my doorstep,
a mole's pink curl of a foot. Last week, cedar
waxwing feathers scattered across the stairs.
Often tiny entrails dot the walk. From a feline
haute cuisine, these leftovers evidence an array
of select entrées. Mouse heart, rabbit tail, and
robin bone, all regale how hunger has its scale.

Mine is weighty with pig and cow, yet delicate
with quail, squid, and snail. So there's pretense
in my palate, for I am aghast when stepping over
the corpse of a half-eaten shrew and I feel quite
saddened by its fate. Then behind my door, I
eat pâté galore. I want my cat's wild instincts
utterly undone, as I cut into my beef Wellington.

ODE

Dead on the double
yellow line that divides Route 202
the skunk is sprawled.
His new winter fur sways and separates
with the onrush of wind and

wheels. How things go round, he doesn't
wonder: never did. Still
I do, wincing at the black and white of it.
His coat, an animal's
luxuriant, is pelted over the asphalt. Varmint,

his stink putrefies the cold air
without compromise. But he is compromised
on this curve of the road. His spirit,
that tireless caricature of odors, has passed
a sleek stripe at breakneck speed.

OUR SECOND AIREDALE

The monk suggests electric shock.
He is a Franciscan; for an hour,
he has listened over long distance.
The trainer tells us to try tranquilizers,
a muzzle, a cage, and consistency.
The canine psychologist says, "Naturally,

you betrayed him. He used to be the baby
and now, no doubt, he's just the dog."
For the vet, it is an old war, fought

again. A kind coercion, domestication is
a slight twisting of the legs upon which
instinct runs, a small severing of the five
senses from the soul, like fingers from
the hand, the paw. The whole thing is a howl.

Trying to teach "an old dog new tricks,"
eventually, we are tied to a tragedy
of manners, a choke chain of choices.

He cannot adjust. Every night he keeps us
awake. He cannot be left, in any way, alone.
Under his fur, under our furniture, he is
so alone. He destroys five doors, but never
escapes. With his teeth, he attacks

a docile bitch, who dies. He resists his last
chance, a new master. When thunder trembles,
he convulses with fear. Then, one quiet after-

noon, as cool air bends the grass over the deep
hole he has dug to elude the hot summer
days, we take him. Indirect, as so many human
plots and meanings, we "have him put to sleep."
Sad masters of obedience and death, we tried
and tried, wanting to be so playful and humane.

DRIED BUTTERFLIES

Things just are.
They outlast the living
who can create them
and mean them to be
more. In time, even
museums are mortal.

So what then is
the connection between
yourself and perhaps
a particular taste or color,
one selected shell from
an entire shore?

Or take the plant
chosen to grow daily
under your unconscious
observance of time and change
though maybe the weather
wills out. Who says
"beautiful" in you
or, more so, "mine"?

I recall dried butterflies,
pressed into transparencies,

found in shoe boxes with shoes
in dead Aunt Gertrude's closet.
No one said anything about them
maybe since she never did,
but it confused an issue
in some confine of the mind,
made mourning more mysterious
as if the coffin were closed
with the person inside still
changing.

We are collectors
gathering information, artifacts,
icons of identification
glass-cased or closet-closed,
signs and symbols of self
on walls, tables, bodies,
in drawers, sheds, and attics.

All paraphernalia of the person
are an adhesion
to the unknown archetype
of ourselves, of who we are
and will have been,
always an inheritance.

MY LATE FATHER'S JUNK MAIL

It arrives daily, promising insights
into the bond market, pest control
(free for the first month), getaway
vacations, subscriptions at discount,

coupons for vacuums, lubes, furnace
cleanings, and tire changes; specials
on cell phones and software. Some-
times, there's even a sample, a small

box of cereal, a single squeeze of tooth-
paste or shampoo. Charities of all sorts
want his donations, his pledge to help
cure disease, elect officials, advance

education, stop extinctions. Each crisis
needs him. And then they want his
opinion too! Surveys and sweepstakes
have his name in letters larger than life

urging him to hurry, rush, and not miss
out. Months ago, ocean waves enveloped
his ashes, but still these piles of paper
come, not even forwarded, just updated

as if he had moved in with me, his dutiful
daughter, who repeats his lambaste against
bureaucracy, advertising, and waste. I write
his rage. Here, postmortem is posthaste.

SEMBLANCE OF REALITY

Often it is not creepy, but
comforting, how the past
breathes in and out of us
without a surprise or start.
Surge and resurgence,

history resuscitates all
its airy ghosts, elusive
and essential as oxygen.
Listen, I tell you they have
presence. And I am not

haunted. I do not gasp or
offer any sentiment. Once
I found my sister though
never caught her eye. I had
a brief reel, so to speak,

with old Roethke. Inadvertent,
I made acquaintance with
William Tecumseh Sherman.
In the rain, I heard Piaf hum.
I just take them as they come.

LAST CALL

After his last coma
my grandfather went off the track
and did not talk of dying
but got a ticket back
to Chicago by half a century
and found a telephone
to call from that train crash
and told Theresa again
he had arrived unharmed
then he hung up
without saying

ELEGY

He went without a cry or a kick,
a blink or a hic. From one sleep, he
slipped into another. Gently
he turned in his fluid existence
until the liquid globe became his
singular struggle and he shifted

the great weight of being. Thus, he was
free from all lessons, languages, and
love. By being less than five hundred
grams of unborn dreams, he escaped
each legislation. Missing even
the morgue, he lay in a bucket where

he was cradled in his circular
fate. To a brain with a microscope,
he donated his bean-sized kidneys;
sticks of bone marrow he bequeathed
to the soul of science. He gave new
flesh to fire and softened the ashes

with innocence. A frenzy of white
spirits, flocking like gulls, gathered
his ghost. He was so unassuming
doing his dervish of life and death,
so lusty in his liberation,
so lost to reconciliation.

HAPPENSTANCE

in memory of Robert H. Dewey

I know the horror show. At six years old,
I heard about the psychopath who butchered
the picnicking family of four, then shot
a policeman, took his uniform, and acted

like the law. My uncle opened the car door
then drove as directed, but soon suspected
something else. Trembling, he dropped
a cigarette onto the car floor and reached

to retrieve it, but the little misshapen
murderer thought he might be going
for a gun. So he shot my uncle and dumped
his dying body into the trunk. In testimony,

the jury heard anecdotes, all the monstrous
cruelty of the murderer's father who often
abandoned the boy to starve for days
in a sealed cave. How one thing finds another

I do not know though I try to be at home
in the haphazard. Amid the daily news
of armies, viruses, and madmen, I act casual
fearing that my children are my prayers.

SMALL BOUQUETS

THE GARDEN GREEN, THE GARDEN GONE

At the last, things grow precious. Finality
will seize your sentiment as a clever actor
will find his light, take his bow. Soon

you will see the landscape glowing into
an emerald, the lawns and leaves bright as ice,
the ocean flaring with an oily gleam. Then

you will watch everything disappear
in the shapes of clouds, in great rockets
of cigar smoke. You will cry out your little

remembrances: the odor of damp trees, the wide
avenue of a great city, the dog and rooster
raising the dawn of a clear day, the afternoon

your mother was so affectionate. You will
question whether your heart still circulates;
you will ask how you devoured love and lost

the courage to live. You will beg dust and
water not to dance a dervish; you will plead
with earth and fire not to abuse each other.

But in the secret chambers of your mind,
you will know the answers, the same answers
you knew when animals rattled their chains and

ate through their own paws, the same answers
you knew when the tortures were televised, when
atrocities became entertainment, when luxury

grew as insistent as a force-feeding machine
crammed down the neck of a goose, when every
belly was distended from too much or too little.

The same answers will stand in your mind, but
they will be just a bit beyond, something
like the space Michelangelo made between

God's hand and Adam's. You will weep at how
you liked to press your luck, how you denied
knowing any alternatives or consequences,

how you wanted to steal apples or wear a crown
without thorns. You will howl disastrous clichés
ultimate understandings, your own name.

THE DICTIONARY
UNDER MOUNTAIN FRINGE

Refers to Allegheny vine or climbing
fumitory, which is delicate, herbaceous,
feathery, and in Colorado, a wormwood,
having racemes full of purplish or
white flowers. Racemes define a simple
inflorescence born along a common
axis from short pedicels. Given access
to lexical pedicels, they are said to
be the ultimate divisions along
a common stalk, which is where I
left the trellis for the cover and said,
"So are we all until we're dead," then
I closed the *Random House* beside my bed.

AN INSOMNIAC'S SYRINGA

She longs for sleep to throw itself at her feet
like a flush-faced boy hurling the evening
news over the mock orange and onto the porch.
She waits for an indelible ink to blot
out the everyday dissertation, to make
a moonscape of the tiresome old neighborhood,
an ether of the atmosphere. But the pure
pillow has been sabotaged by a sly
perfume. An orange white blossom dupes her dream,
douses charcoal with cream, and turns old-fashioned
flowers into hybrids of false hope. Wanting
only an oblivion to come, she lies
still, listening for one more boy, bicycling
past, one sweet mockery of slumber, at last.

BEGINNING

Beginning to forget, every day it's something
else. Now I have left the shovel and shears
in the rain. At the window, I watch the soft
water loosening each wooden handle from

its metal edge. These apprehensions gather
into a bouquet, my rosebuds of dismay. Soon
the saturated poppies will be left as stalks
and the dahlias' pink heads will hang, drowned

in the fluid of their birth. My garden severs
to join, cuts to connect. I confuse clouds with
clocks, mind with memory. I forget blades
are not grips. I forget how fast blood drips.

THE LOTUS FLOATS

Past sedges, rushes, and reeds beyond the yellow flags,
Saint-John's-worts, and water arum, above the larvae
of leech and mayfly, the miry egg masses of snails
and common frog spawn, under the midday sky, its single
cloud passing over the pond as a diving beetle darts
through the vaporous image blurring the egret's stark
legs and the sticklebacks' quivers, rooted in mud, yet
immaculate with light, water lilies rose with myth.
Ancients worshiped them, buoyant brides, natant nymphs.

MY OLD CRIMSON GERANIUM

At the desk, I longed for a kill
fee. The numbered days, their grid
and maze, grew relentlessly. Lines
with deadlines went round the black

roller as my story unwound with
lettered keys to pound the doors of
memory down. Promises and ribbons
kept breaking. Truth was a risk.

"Worth taking?" I asked the flower
at my side. "What if I just lied?"
Flaming out of a cracked clay pot
by a grated window, its pane hot

a match-head petal fell like a word
and lit an answer as if to be heard.

EIGHT ZINNIAS

First I must ask you to see her homely farmhouse
kitchen with its prefab paneling and rust-stained
sink, detergent bottles and rubber drainboard,
the plastic wall clock and dairy co-op calendar.
Now take a look over there at the mammoth deep
freeze, a sarcophagus of an appliance, bearing
its frozen body of food as if the entombment of all
appetite. Still something else seizes your eye

and insists you focus on the center of the oil-
cloth table. Now you stare as their bristly stems
flare out of the mouth of their Mason jar: hot
pink, Naples yellow, purple, xanthic white, magenta,
aureate, vermilion, and cadmium orange, each one
answering the vivid though inexplicable desire
for beauty, each one the fervid blossoming of her
land, each one a perfection from an arthritic hand.

NE-M'OUBLIEZ-PAS*

In an effort to see visions, the Egyptians anointed
their eyes with these specks of azure and cerulean blue. I too
have seen the minuscule petals swirl their millefiori blur
over each iris, dizzying as a water globe shaken so

bits of sapphire and lapis lazuli excite small blizzards
of blue, scattering the sky, flurries of Seurat's empyreal
dots. Covered with the confetti of such illusions, one may
forget these discs are floral footnotes, remembered asterisks.

*Also known as mouse-ear, scorpion grass, and forget-me-not.

TO AN AMARYLLIS BULB

Hidden in your brown papery heft, you could remain
as respectable as a rutabaga, but you are not
horticulture's recluse. In fact, your ambitions are
utterly profuse. Even in this modest encasement

your exoticism cannot be contained, and thus you slide
the small tips of your green porcelain tongues out
to the light. Botanists call these slick protrusions
"scapes." More to the point, they are your escapes,

for these jaded slips tell remarkably who you are:
an astonishment of transformation, asserting that
one can go far. From a peasant girl bound in sack-
cloth, you emerge an outrageous red-satin movie star.

MONOLOGUE OF AN AMARYLLIS

Even Virgil in his *Eclogues* entertained
my emanations. I was his shepherdess! But
never one to flock or follow, I soon went
from his bucolic Bella to a Bella Donna.
(Every pasture needs a little poison.) So
next thing I knew, I grew to have another
name. I became the Naked Lady whose staff
would not keep from growing, going, until
my big Brancusian bud became something
all too certain: one Freudian monolithic
assertion! How I love hyperbole. No shrinking
violet in me. I force my way making winter
act like May. Well rehearsed, I know exactly
when to burst, opening up big and pink
as a girl wanting too much to please
or in silky harlot red I look like pleasure
risking disease. Women envy me
for I am a funnel of bright extremes,
more colorful than their wildest dreams.
I'm the only flower that stops them in
their tracks for I've the accessibility all
human forms lack. I am without chastity. Open
and exquisite, I'm a nectary of pure audacity.

SMALL ALCHEMIES

For thousands of years in ancient Crete, astonishing
transmutations would repeat. Every October in the deadened
autumn grasses, *Crocus sativus* bloomed in flaming masses;
the Minoans plucked their brilliant center pieces, crushing
a golden dust which releases from the female enigma
of this flower's petaloid stigma: saffron. Wondrous spice,
dye, cure–all, and scent, this powder became gold's equivalent
enabling the Minoans to live splendidly until they vanished
in 1100 B.C. This modest flower seeded in its brown button
corm had made alchemy its norm by transforming 4000 stigmas
from kiln to cake, one ounce worth more than gold could make
in Mediterranean marketplaces. How much time erases. Now
that crocus which fired the world long ago is ignored as if
it were lost in snow, alloyed to March and the status quo.

A HAND-TO-MOUTH EXISTENCE

If not often in your life, but only sometimes
or just a meager one time, take the season
from your fingers to your lips. Pluck fiddle-

heads, green and bracken, from their stems.
Break each tender shoot and stalk at its first
moist burst. Let the berries brim in the straw

crown of your overturned hat, warm tomatoes
weigh deep in the arc of your apron, or heap
clams into the overflowing brine of your bucket.

Every season has its sacraments. The sickle
pear falls, ripe with the gravity of change.
Each apple you can reach will ready you for that

first swallow of snow, the tongue tasting so
cold and crystalline. Devour any chance you have
before you are fed to this earth that feeds you.

SUMMER SCENES

THE FORGE

Casco Bay, Maine

White gears of the air, the gulls shriek and revolve while
the water, a frayed and broken belt, slaps between its pulleys
and fabricates the beach. Over the bay, the foundry thuds
its molten tonnage and thuds again. Each August evening
amid brine and birch, sumac and sea grass, shoes and sleep,
this iron weight gravitates toward our summery hearts and
pounds. Its rhythm, a last reminder, resolves that we are
between an anvil and a breath, that we are in the space
where the latch is ajar, that the moon's face is more constant
than we are. On the porch, as our screens recede into thin
castings of the night and the heavy bells of ringing buoys
grow faint, we begin another supper, another joke about
how to silence the foundry, how to keep sand off the steps,
how to empty the vacuum. End over end, we turn a spoon
until it becomes our caliper, mapping the check tablecloth
from cup to knife. We chart the nautical miles between Little
Diamond and our dock, between what is real and is not. Now
the cruise boat nears. Hurrying to the door, we speak of Fellini,
the scene in *Amarcord:* villagers in fog and fishing boats
awaiting the great white liner, the vision that vanishes. Soon
the dishes are done and, one by one, we go to bed where
welded to the dark is every sound, spoken and unsaid.

AUGUST ISLAND

I

Chokeberries blaze in the bush. Rose
hips harden into rubescent beads and birch
bark curls its small scrolls, each white
document marked with an illegible ink,
riddles of the tree. Somewhere time waits
on this August afternoon as summer sucks in
a last hot breath to hold. Goldenrod grows warm
with the weeds and sumac ignites its crimson
torches against all the cold to come. How
impossible to believe that the window will
overwhelm the wasp, the cornflowers fade
into the field, falling and flattening with leaves
and the last moth, flutter and freeze.

II

In the hot calm of sand at low tide, he lies
without wonderment or worry, asleep in the sun.
His arms are outstretched, skin glowing, nearing
a burn; his hair bleached and whorled with salt.
Flecks of mica, obsidian, and ash glimmer in random
ellipses over his heart, each small swell of breath
in his body. In this great stellar light, our side
of midnight, his dreams are blood bright as if
each eyelid were a red gel over a theater Fresnel.
How to hold this warm vision sprawled here
on our little beach among its burnished swimmers,
patchwork of towels, the impassioned digging

of children and dogs? When the waves are held
for a few hours in abeyance, one believes that
the mind might prevail against its own obscurity,
an old lighthouse illuminating new fog, a winter
denying its end rhyme, refusing its epilogue.

III
Pressed against the page, each photo is sealed
under a transparent sheet. Now we look
back to believe that the boat was in the water
and we were in the boat. We see ourselves,
brown-faced strangers in straw hats with self-
conscious smiles. These are our exposures
and, after the negatives, they are all we have.
I remember how no one could find the camera
on that chill gray day after the storm; how
we walked the beach, stooping for bits of blue
glass, sidestepping dead gulls, the wreckage
of lobster traps, the gnarled lines, and tangled
kelp. We were so cold and shaken. Everything
stood in opposition to what we had rented,
what we had wanted, as if summer had
assaulted itself. The big porch was bleak,
the airy bedroom somber. In our album,
I see these images more clearly than if
they were there. Unseasonable and certain,
they appear, truth and its transparencies.

WATERCOLOR

Surges of clouds pelted the waves, drenching daylight
into submission. In an expanse of anguish,
its own inclemency, he reached into the rain
searching to define one watery line, his hand
in the deluge. He stood and withstood those torrents
streaking his vision, flooding his eyes, outpourings
upon an ocean, where pain salted wet paint and
passion, that classical suffering, joined
summer to squall. All in an hour, it was his:
pluvial, dark, intense, even desirable.

OFF STANDARD TIME

Each day as the pendulum of light lengthened
and the cow flicked her straggly tail just a little
farther across her buzzing back, the question
of which way to turn the clocks came closer.
In preparation, my grandmother divided the hour
into ten-minute segments and began her gradual
adjustment six days in advance. "A bit biblical,"

she smiled, "my method is." Lying in the long summer
shadows, I wondered at the elusive time termed
"savings" and the way my grandmother moved her hands.
One afternoon, leaning my silhouette over an earthy bed,
I watched black ants invade a perfect white peony.
My grandmother held my moist shoulder and said, "Enough
to make you sick, but we all tick that way a bit."

SUMMER STORM

Birds hush. A dense calm weights the air. Across
the steamy lawn, shadows darken. Branches
undulate with an ominous grace. Clouds
converge into friction. Over the hills,
thunder sounds, solemn bombs from a foreign
war. Sealing the sills, forcing the sashes
down, I move among my windows. Twelve-over-
twelves are the uneven panes that light this
old Colonial; one farmer's hand-hewn
fortress against the wickedness of New
England weather. And there, hanging on a peg,
is everything, though it is just a straw

hat, my daughter's first hat. The pink grosgrain
streamers stir with the air. Touching the crown,
I can almost hold her head, so bright and new.
Caught in the interweaving of the brim
is one luminous strand, one hair of lightning.
(By a hair, I hold her so and let her go. . . .)
Now the downpour comes. Faintly, I hear her
laughing, wanting to go outside, rattling
the doorknob. Three years old and eager for
atmosphere, she runs bareheaded toward
all the storms to come, believing the world's
inclemencies are only playful ones.

WHEN SHE SLEEPS

Eliza, at eleven

The soul of Bernini stirs, enters
the room, and revels at her bedside
to behold such superlative form. This
adolescent androgyny, the figure

flung into its own dark awakening,
makes Michelangelo moan wanting
to hold the moment in marble. Worthy
of a renaissance beyond her own, she

assumes these poses every night,
modeling even the sheets for a lost
masterpiece. Resurrected, Rodin
stares through the shadows longing

to transcend each outstretched limb
as Lachaise barges in to see this bronze
given to oblivion. Maillol almost
touches the tossled hair but is taken

aback by Brancusi, who claims these
shapes to be abstract. Each vision
departs, an unchiseled dream, and she
is left to herself, a magnum opus unseen.

JELLYFISH

Moving its translucent mass through the watery
shadows of the dock and then, past the dock (some-
thing so real which now is not), the jellyfish
swam in its slow float while we (I and my daughter,
then just three) ran back and forth predicting that limp
pink gleam and each embodiment it would seem.

"A jello umbrello!" she began and turned
to me expectantly. Censoring (an after-
birth, broken veins, or Medusa's myth, the monstrous
queen made mortal and mother), I stood in silence
until it ended with a shout: the jelly-
fish glided out. Now months have passed, but surprise!

"The jellyfish was in my eyes!" Caroline calls
while caught between depth and surface of a dream.
"It bleeded and it singed!" Her conjugations
soon will exact simple irregularities
and tensing will be not verbs but time's tentacles
untangling her parachute, waving at me.

BY HEART

DAILIES & RUSHES

As a stunted woman (you might say
stunt) my body is everyday
ready to explode in some crazy way.
My breasts feel wired, patched with squibs.
I'll take bruises, cuts, a few cracked ribs.
Ready for jumps, rolls, even ad libs,
I want some action, to get real hot.
Stars get millions, but I'll take squat.
Falling into flames, I cry, "Why? Why not?"

THIRTEEN BY THIRTEEN

Immeasurable distances describe love like light-
years crossing a café table, interstates joining
for instance Ohio to Arizona, foreign
letters, the Orient Express bringing the full moon
to pull brain waves into high tide, a turbulence
of longing. I ask where does one draw the line as this
expanse consumes me, its magnitude grown menacing,
my pulse becoming seismographic. The real point is
lost in arrows—classic as Cupid's, excessive as
Sebastian's—stabbing at all definition, each
piercing insistence that the heart cannot divide
its eager edges from ultimate aches. Love unites
chance and fate. So come now, be my triumph, my mistake.

HALF NOTE

Next to each other, it's secrets we want
to share, closing the distance between bed

and chair, dark as the path turning our steps
in the night, deep as Scarlatti played

without light. When the body begins its
counterpoint to the brain, rhythms grow harder

and harder to train. For days, I withheld
one hand from you. But one-handed, your music

played through, touching me, as if by two.

IGNITING

We rub and rub sticks together
all day. Persistently, I say
nothing changes faster than fire.
Continually, he asks what
is more certain than the sun
inserting itself in the sea.
Slowly, the golden coin drops, lost
in a lapping slot. Dying flames
insinuate themselves in us.
A phosphorescence turns to ash.
I ask him what he will do when
I am ash. He answers, "I will
spread you over the waves like fire."

FARTHER THAN THIS

I wish we could go farther than this walk
to a distance by turns and inclines, unfamiliar
signs, days of remote vistas, panoramas in excess
of probability, landscapes where all likelihood

could not lead us. We would find our way there by
wandering in an amplitude of imagination
on a path we could no more promote than follow,
the first step, headfirst, an oblique sublimity.

HOUSE LIGHTS DOWN

In the straight-back wooden chairs of eternity left
from a recent run of *Our Town,* I sit beside you
to tell the darkness how we endure endless forfeiture,
how our days disappear, how all we do must be left
undone. As on a pocket watch that never opens its face,
the unregarded hours elude us and convey seconds

into seasons, making a surrealism of years. Already we have
not walked far enough in snow, swum deep enough in the lake.
We haven't read a week of Keats or memorized seven
minutes of Mahler. Will we ever pick a wild peach, step
on shadows in Sicily or stones in the Bering Sea?
All unlikely. Like bees abandoning an autumn field,

we yield, relinquishing our nightclothes and notebooks, the lost
powdery scent of our missing infant, the dazzling waltz,
the daily bread and the best words, left unsaid. Ours is this
small space between an answered prayer and a coming
curse. Still, we are honored to have played our part, lovers
living our days unrehearsed, as if each were the first.